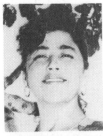

Isabel Felix Leon
DOB: 02/24/57
Sex: F
Race: White/Hisp
Height: 5'2"
Weight: 125 lbs
Hair: Brown
Eyes: Brown

Speaks English w/strong accent as well as Spanish. Silver streaks in hair. May go by Isabel L. Sandige.

William Bruno Leon Sandige
Missing: 10/22/94
Age Now: 2yr
Missing From: Phoenix, AZ
DOB: 10/5/93
Age Disap: 12 mo
Sex: M
Race: White/Hisp
Height: 2'6"
Weight: 30lbs
Hair: Brown
Eyes: Blue

Abducted by mother Isabel Felix Leon.

Margaret Isabel L. Sandige
Missing: 10/22/94
Age Now: 7 yr
Missing From: Phoenix, AZ
DOB: 9/16/88
Age Disap: 6 yr
Sex: F
Race: White/Hisp
Height: 3'7"
Weight: 46 lbs
Hair: Brown
Eyes: Blue

Speaks Spanish & English. Abducted by mother Isabel Felix Leon.

Sarah Natasha Coleman
Missing: 08/28/94
Age Now: 11 yr
Missing From: Phoenix, AZ
DOB: 8/4/84
Age Disap: 10 yr
Sex: F
Race: Black
Height: 4'5"
Weight: 75 lbs
Hair: Brown
Eyes: Brown

1" scar under left eye, round burn scar on wrist. Abducted by mother, Monica Godfrey.

Monica Linda Godfrey
DOB: 10/02/64
Sex: F
Race: Black
Height: 5'5"
Weight: 127 lbs
Hair: Brown
Eyes: Brown

May wear hazel contact lenses. Scar/blemish on forehead.

Jacquelina Ann Gomez
Missing: 04/20/92
Age Now: 7 yr
Missing From: Chicago, IL
DOB: 9/10/88
Age Disap: 3 yr
Sex: F
Race: White
Height: 3'2"
Weight: 34 lbs
Hair: Brown
Eyes: Brown

When last seen missing two front teeth. Abducted by father, Ramon Gomez.

Ramon Gomez
DOB: 07/23/63
Sex: M
Race: White
Height: 5'8"
Weight: 210 lbs
Hair: Black
Eyes: Brown

Randell Lamar Henderson
DOB: 06/25/55
Sex: M
Race: White
Height: 5'8"
Weight: 130 lbs
Hair: Brown
Eyes: Blue-green

Alias: Randy Henderson. Scar between eyes, chipped front tooth, rose tattoo on lower left arm, pierced left ear. May be known as Ran Henderson.

Roman Lamar Henderson
Missing: 06/05/94
Age Now: 9 yr
Missing From: Miami, FL
DOB: 2/15/86
Age Disap: 8 yr
Sex: M
Race: White
Height: 4'
Weight: 56 lbs
Hair: Blonde
Eyes: Blue

Small scar near eyebrow, freckles on nose & cheeks, pierced left ear, brown birthmark on back of right thigh. Abducted by father, Randell Lamar Henderson.

Yemane Cyril Hughes
Missing: 07/26/94
Age Now: 3 yr
Missing From: Houston, TX
DOB: 11/8/92
Age Disap: 20 mo
Sex: M
Race: Black
Height: 2'6"
Weight: 35 lbs
Hair: Black
Eyes: Brown

Small birthmark on left side of back near shoulder. Dimples in each cheek. Nickname "Monty". Abducted by father, David Parks.

David Griffin Parks
DOB: 04/29/62
Sex: M
Race: Black
Height: 6'1"
Weight: 149 lbs
Hair: Black
Eyes: Brown

Small mole on left side of nose. Balding but may have hair in dreadlocks.

 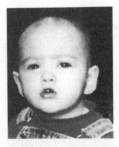

Patricia Joan O'Byrne
DOB: 10/16/57
Sex: F
Race: White
Height: 6'1"
Weight: 210 lbs
Hair: Brown
Eyes: Green

Faint scar on upper lip.

Sigourney Teresa Chisholm
Missing: 05/31/93
Age Now: 4 yr
Missing From: Toronto, Ontario, CN
DOB: 09/20/91
Age Disap: 20 mo
Sex: F
Race: White
Height: 2'8"
Weight: 22 lbs
Hair: Brown
Eyes: Brown

May be known as Sigourney O'Byrne. Goes by nickname "Sigi". Abducted by mother, Patricia Joan O'Byrne.

Julia Esther Arellano
DOB: 02/13/54
Sex: F   **Race:** White/Hisp
Height: 5'2"   **Weight:** 120 lbs
Hair: Brown   **Eyes:** Hazel

Alias: Julia Esther Urbina or Julia Esther Carrillo Alonso.

Elizabeth M. Arellano
Missing: 07/23/91   **Age Now:** 10 yr
Missing From: Manitoba, CN
DOB: 02/26/85   **Age Disap:** 6 yr
Sex: F   **Race:** White/Hisp
Height: 3'5"   **Weight:** 44 lbs
Hair: Brown   **Eyes:** Blue

Abducted by mother, Julia Esther Arellano.

Walter Ricardo Arellano
Missing: 07/23/91   **Age Now:** 14 yr
Missing From: Manitoba, CN
DOB: 10/7/81   **Age Disap:** 9 yr
Sex: M   **Race:** White/Hisp
Height: 4'5"   **Weight:** 73 lbs
Hair: Brown   **Eyes:** Brown

Wears glasses, scar on right eyebrow.
Abducted by mother, Julia Esther Arellano.

Ashley Marie Dalton
Missing: 11/13/94   **Age Now:** 5 yr
Missing From: Richmond, VA
DOB: 07/12/90   **Age Disap:** 4 yr
Sex: F   **Race:** White
Height: 3'7"   **Weight:** 48 lbs
Hair: Brown   **Eyes:** Blue

Abducted by mother, Tara Marie Gomes.

Tara Marie Gomes
DOB: 10/21/71
Sex: F   **Race:** White/Hisp
Height: 5'6"   **Weight:** 160 lbs
Hair: Brown   **Eyes:** Hazel

Facial scars, may walk with a limp. May be wearing glasses. Front teeth crowded together.

Adel Bjiouat
Missing: 07/6/94   **Age Now:** 7 yr
Missing From: Raytown, MO
DOB: 12/17/87   **Age Disap:** 6 yr
Sex: M   **Race:** White
Height: 4'0"   **Weight:** 50 lbs
Hair: Black   **Eyes:** Brown

Nickname is Del. Abducted by father, Khalid Bjiouat.

Khalid Bjiouat
DOB: 12/4/63
Sex: M   **Race:** White
Height: 6'2""   **Weight:** 170 lbs
Hair: Black   **Eyes:** Brown
Has a moustache, possibly a goatee.

Sharon Francis Schild
DOB: 12/17/46
Sex: F   **Race:** White
Height: 5'9"   **Weight:** 120 lbs
Hair: Blonde   **Eyes:** Green

Stephanie Marie Schild
Missing: 10/02/89   **Age Now:** 9 yr
Missing From: Cincinnati, OH
DOB: 11/2/86   **Age Disap:** 2 yr
Sex: F   **Race:** White
Height: 2'10"   **Weight:** 35 lbs
Hair: Blonde   **Eyes:** Blue

Hair brownish-blonde. Abducted by mother, Sharon Francis Schild.

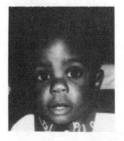 

Oscar Oblajura Emeasoba
Missing: 08/17/92   **Age Now:** 4 yr
Missing From: Silver Spring, MD
DOB: 03/20/91   **Age Disap:** 17 mo
Sex: M   **Race:** Black
Height: 2'0"   **Weight:** 28 lbs
Hair: Black   **Eyes:** Brown

Small black birthmark on upper leg. Abducted by father, Augustine Emeosoba.

Augustine Okechuckwu Emeasoba
DOB: 12/24/42
Sex: M   **Race:** Black
Height: 5'8"   **Weight:** 200 lbs
Hair: Black/grey   **Eyes:** Brown

Large mouth & nose, scars on hands and feet.

Robert Edward Maloney
Missing: 03/1/94   **Age Now:** 12 yr
Missing From: San Jose, CA
DOB: 03/04/83   **Age Disap:** 11 yr
Sex: M   **Race:** White/Hisp
Height: 5'0"   **Weight:** 90 lbs
Hair: Blonde   **Eyes:** Green

May be in company of non-custodial father.

Kali Ann Poulton
Missing: 05/23/94   **Age Now:** 6 yr
Missing From: East Rochester, NY
DOB: 09/20/89   **Age Disap:** 4 yr
Sex: F   **Race:** White
Height: 4'0"   **Weight:** 40 lbs
Hair: Blonde   **Eyes:** Blue

Small light brown moles on each side of face by lower jaw. Pierced ears.

Patriotic SYMBOLS ACTIVITY BOOK

Author	Linda Milliken
Editor	Kathy Rogers
Design	Mary Jo Keller
Illustrator	Barb Lorseyedi

© 1996 **EDUPRESS** • P.O. Box 883 • Dana Point, CA 92629

ISBN 1-56472-075-6

Table of Contents

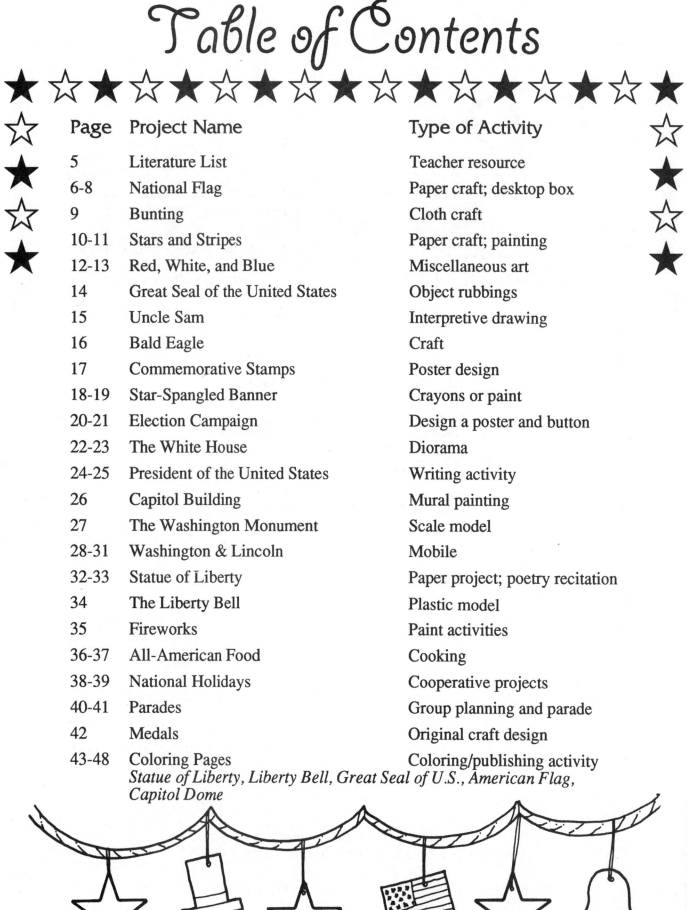

Literature List

• **Honest Abe**
by Edith Kunhardt;
Greenwillow LB 1993. (PS-3)
Folk art helps to create this picture book
version of Lincoln's life.

• **A Picture Book of George Washington**
by David A. Adler;
Holiday LB 1989. (PS-3)
A picture biography of America's first
president.

• **A Flag for Our Country**
by Eve Spencer;
Raintree LB 1993. (K-3)
The story of how Betsy Ross made the
first American flag.

• **The Story of the White House**
by Kate Waters;
Scholastic 1991. (K-3)
This photo essay gives a history of the
White House, describing the layout as
well as individual rooms.

• **The Inside-Outside Book of
Washington, D.C.**
by Roxie Munro;
Dutton 1987. (1-3)
Views inside and outside the familiar
buildings of Washington, D.C.

• **The Flag of the United States**
by Dennis B. Fradin;
Childrens LB 1989. (2-3)
How this important symbol of America
came to be.

• **Lady With a Torch: How the Statue of
Liberty Was Born**
by Eleanor Coerr;
Harper LB 1986. (2-4)
How the statue was constructed along
with details on the sculptor Bartholdi.

• **A Memorial for Mr. Lincoln**
by Brent Ashabrenner;
Putnam 1992. (2-4)
This book chronicles the building of the
Lincoln Memorial and includes
information on Lincoln's life.

• **District of Columbia: In Words and
Pictures**
by Kathryn Wentzel Lumley;
Childrens LB 1981. (2-4)
Historical and geographical information
about America's capitol.

• **The Story of the Capitol**
by Marilyn Prolman;
Childrens LB 1969. (4-6)
The history and architecture of the
nation's capitol.

• **Lincoln's Birthday**
by Dennis B. Fradin;
Enslow LB 1990. (3-5)
Covers background and customs of this
national holiday.

• **Washington's Breakfast**
by Jean Fritz;
Putnam LB 1969. (3-5)
George W. Allen knows all there is to
know about our first president—except
what he had for breakfast.

• **The Story of the Liberty Bell**
by Natalie Miller;
Childrens LB 1969. (4-6)
The story of one of our country's most
famous symbols.

• **The Statue of Liberty**
by Leonard Everett Fisher;
Holiday LB 1985. (4-6)
The story of the statue and its presentation
to America by the French people.

National Flag

★ Historical Aid

Probably the most important patriotic symbol is the national flag which represents the land, people, and government of the United States.

On June 14, 1777, the Continental Congress resolved that "the Flag of the United States be 13 stripes alternate red and white, and the Union be 13 stars white in a blue field representing a new constellation." But Congress did not indicate how the stars should be arranged, so flagmakers used various designs.

In the years that followed, various Presidents sometimes proclaimed new arrangements for the stars when a new state entered the Union. In some cases, the army and navy worked out the new designs. Presidential orders fixed the positions of the stars in 1912, for 48 stars, and in 1960, for 50.

Project

Form cooperative groups to create paper flags that illustrate changes in the national flag over the last 200 years.

Materials

- Flag cards, following
- Red, white and blue butcher paper
- Ruler or other measuring tool
- Scissors   • Glue

Directions

1. Divide into eight cooperative groups.

2. Cut apart the flag cards and give one to each group. Explain the color key.

   red

   blue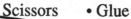

3. Each group assigns tasks: measure, sketch, cut, and glue. Determine the finished size of the flag before beginning.

4. Follow the flag illustration on the card to recreate a paper flag.

5. When the flags are complete, compare the similarities and differences. Create a display for the school entry, office, or cafeteria.

☆ Continental Colors ☆
America's first national flag—1775-1777

☆ Flag of 1777 ☆
By Congressional Resolution—1777-1795

☆ Flag of 1777 ☆
Rarely used circle design—1777

☆ Flag of 1795 ☆
15 stars and stripes for 15 states—1795

☆ Flag of 1818 ☆
13 stripes and a star for each state—1818

☆ Great Star Flag ☆
Used occasionally—1818

☆ 48-Star Flag ☆
Served longer than any other—1912-1959

☆ 50-Star Flag ☆
The current flag—1960-present

National Flag Projects

Here are some unusual ways to recreate the National Flag.

★ ★ ★ Paper Chain Flag ★ ★ ★

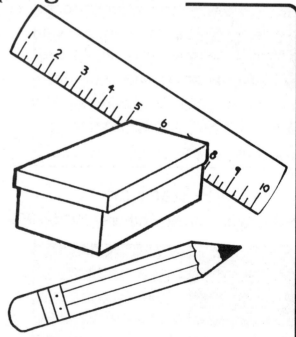

Materials:
- Red, white, blue construction paper
- Star pattern (page 11)
- Scissors • Glue
- Ruler • Pencil

Directions:
1. Measure and cut paper into 2 x 5-inch (5 x 12.7 cm) strips.
2. Create paper chains with the strips. Each chain should be the same color.
3. Assemble the chains in rows on the classroom wall to create the national flag. Staple the chains in place at several points. Cut stars to glue on.

★ ★ ★ Box Top Flag ★ ★ ★

Materials:
- Rectangular-shaped gift box
- Red, white, blue tissue paper
- Scissors • Starch
- Ruler • Pencil

Directions:
1. Measure and mark lines on the box top to duplicate the national flag.
2. Cut tissue paper into small squares. Brush them in place on the box top with starch slightly diluted with water.
3. Allow the lid to dry completely. Use the box as desktop storage.

Bunting

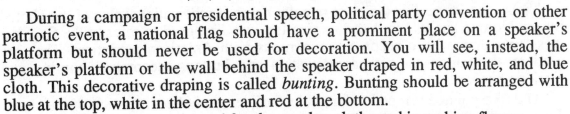

★ Historical Aid

During a campaign or presidential speech, political party convention or other patriotic event, a national flag should have a prominent place on a speaker's platform but should never be used for decoration. You will see, instead, the speaker's platform or the wall behind the speaker draped in red, white, and blue cloth. This decorative draping is called *bunting*. Bunting should be arranged with blue at the top, white in the center and red at the bottom.

Bunting is also the term used for the woolen cloth used in making flags.

Project

Make bunting to drape and decorate the classroom walls. This project should be done outside on a grassy area.

Materials

- Old white sheets or cloth
- Red and blue dye
- Disposable plastic gloves
- Clothesline or rope
- Large buckets or tubs
- Clothespins
- Masking tape
- Fabric scissors

Directions

1. Assign children into work groups, each having a different responsibility in the dyeing process. All participating children should wear plastic gloves.

2. Cut the sheets or cloth in strips about 12-inches (30.48 cm) wide.

3. Follow the directions on the package to make batches of red and blue dye in several buckets. Leave some buckets empty for transporting dyed cloth strips and for rinsing.

4. One group dyes the cloth strips. Another rinses the strips. A third hangs them to dry.

5 Together, drape the dry cloth strips on the wall, blue on top, red on the bottom. Hold the cloth in place with masking tape.

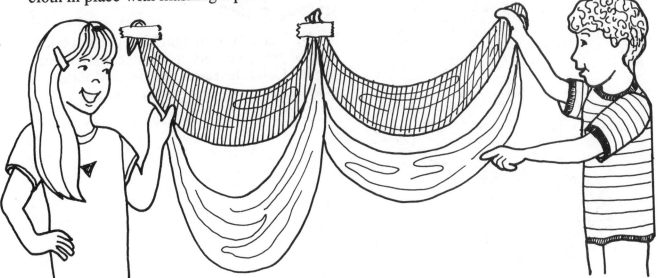

Stars and Stripes

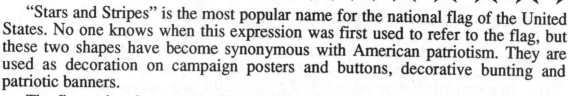

★ Historical Aid

"Stars and Stripes" is the most popular name for the national flag of the United States. No one knows when this expression was first used to refer to the flag, but these two shapes have become synonymous with American patriotism. They are used as decoration on campaign posters and buttons, decorative bunting and patriotic banners.

The five-pointed star and red and blue stripes symbolize the union of the states. They represent the land, the people, the government of the United States and the ideals upon which the country was founded.

Project

Choose one or more of the art and craft ideas to make projects featuring stars and stripes. The materials you will need appear in bold type.

Ceiling Stars

Trace the large **star pattern** on **white poster board.** Use **scissors** to cut around the outline. Use a **hole punch** to make holes at half-inch (1.27 cm) intervals around the outer edge of the star. Lace through the holes with **red or blue yarn** as shown. Use yarn to hang the stars varying distances from the ceiling.

Yikes! Stripes

Use **red and blue crayons** to create a striped design on **white construction paper**. Use **scissors** and **star patterns** to cut a **red, white or blue construction paper** star. **Glue** the star to pop-off the edge of the striped paper.

Group Stars

Use **red and blue marking pens** to trace several **star patterns** on **white construction paper.** Color the stars with **red and blue crayons** to create designs and patterns.

Red, White, and Blue

★ Historical Aid

Red, white, and blue. These three colors have become symbolic representatives of American patriotism.

The Continental Congress left no record to show why it chose red, white, and blue as the colors for the American flag. In 1782, the Congress of the Confederation also chose these colors for the Great Seal of the United States. The resolution on the seal listed the meanings for the colors:

Red—for hardiness and courage.

White—for purity and innocence.

Blue—for vigilance, perseverance, and justice.

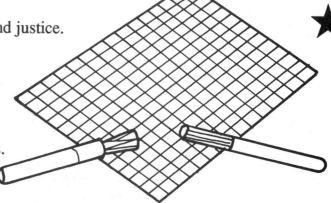

Project

Choose from the following projects to dress up the classroom in patriotic colors.

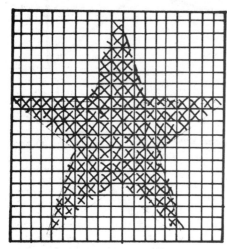

Cross-Stitch Sampler

Use **thin-tipped, red, white, and blue marking pens** to create a cross-stitch design on **graphing paper**.

Patriotic Garland

Cut patriotic shapes from **red, white, and blue construction paper**. Use a **hole-punch** to make a hole at the top of each shape. Use **string** to tie the shapes on **thick yarn** to create a garland to drape across the classroom walls or ceiling.

Crepe-paper Windsock

Cut a **poster board** strip and **staple** the ends together to form a circle.

Cut and **tape** strips of alternating **red, white, and blue crepe paper** to the inside of the circle.

Staple another poster board strip to the circle to create a handle. Hang from the ceiling.

Ribbon Rally

Start with a **white paper plate**. Use glue to decorate the paper plate with **red, white, and blue curling ribbon, satin ribbon, trims** and **bows**.

Tape the plates side-by-side on the classroom wall to spell out the letters U.S.A.

Yarn Swirls

Cut lengths of thick **red, white, and blue yarn**.

Cover a construction paper square by gluing the yarn in circular patterns and swirls.

Great Seal of the United States

  ★ Historical Aid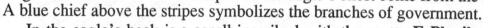

The government adopted the *Great Seal of the United States* on June 20, 1782. It is used to authenticate important documents. The seal features an eagle, symbolizing self-reliance. It holds an olive branch with 13 leaves and olives in its right talon, and 13 arrows in its left, symbolizing a country that desires peace but has the ability to wage war. Thirteen vertical stripes on the eagle's chest come from the flag of 1777. A blue chief above the stripes symbolizes the branches of government.

In the eagle's beak is a scroll inscribed with the motto **E Pluribus Unum** (*ee PLOO rih bus YOO num*), a Latin phrase meaning "out of many," referring to the creation of one nation from 13 colonies. Benjamin Franklin, John Adams, and Thomas Jefferson, members of the seal committee, suggested the motto. Since 1873, law requires that this motto appear on one side of every United States coin minted.

Project

Create coin rubbings that reveal the motto of the Great Seal of the United States.

Materials

- Plain white paper
- Red or blue crayons
- Coins

 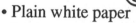

Directions

1. Place a coin under the white paper.

2. Rub a crayon back and forth over spot on the paper that the coin is under. The image of the coin will appear on the paper.

3. Lift the paper and place another coin in a different location under the paper. Choose a crayon and repeat step #2.

4. Continue to change the coin and move it to a different spot under the paper. Alternate the crayon color.

Uncle Sam

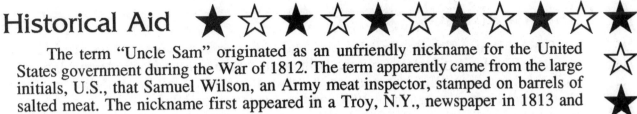

★ Historical Aid

The term "Uncle Sam" originated as an unfriendly nickname for the United States government during the War of 1812. The term apparently came from the large initials, U.S., that Samuel Wilson, an Army meat inspector, stamped on barrels of salted meat. The nickname first appeared in a Troy, N.Y., newspaper in 1813 and spread rapidly.

The costume of Uncle Sam, decorated with stars and stripes, originated in the cartoons of the 1830s. His image appeared on many patriotic posters urging men to enlist in the military and women to work in defense plants during World Wars I and II. In 1961, Congress passed a resolution recognizing Uncle Sam as a national symbol.

Project

Use listening skills and draw an original interpretation of Uncle Sam's image.

Materials

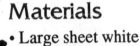

• Large sheet white construction paper
• Crayons

Directions

1. Do not share any pictures of Uncle Sam prior to beginning this activity!

2. Read the descriptive phrases of Uncle Sam that appear in the box below.

3. Give students time to respond to each one, drawing the image of what they hear on the white construction paper.

4. Compare illustrations. How many different Uncle Sams appear in the drawings?

Uncle Sam

1. Draw the face of a man who has dark eyes and a pointed nose.

2. Add a gray beard and gray bushy hair.

3. Put a tall white hat on his head.

4. Make red and blue stripes and white stars on the hat.

5. Put a bow tie around his neck.

6. Put him in a dark blue coat with shiny yellow buttons.

7. Put red and white striped pants on him.

Bald Eagle

★ Historical Aid

The eagle is a fierce, powerful bird and has long been viewed as a symbol of freedom. The United States chose the bald eagle, found only in North America, as its national bird in 1782. The species has been protected by federal law in the continental United States since 1940, and in Alaska since 1953.

A bald eagle may measure 30 to 35 inches (76 to 89 cm) long from the bill to the tip of the tail. It weighs from 8 to 13 pounds (3.6 to 5.9 kg). The head is covered with feathers. The long wing feathers are strong and stiff. Bald eagles have strong legs and feet with powerful talons (claws). The beak is over an inch (2.54 cm) long. Most eagles are dark brown or black. The tail feathers and head feathers are white. A bald eagle builds a nest called an eyrie, usually in a tall tree near water. They use the same eyrie every year.

Project

Use recycled materials to create a dimensional bald eagle.

Materials

- White meat or produce trays
- Half-sheet red or blue construction paper
- Brown, black, and yellow tempera paint
- Pencil
- Scissors
- Glue
- Paint brush

Directions

1. Using the illustration as a guide, draw the basic shape of a bald eagle on the chalkboard.

2. Students duplicate the drawing by cutting shapes from the meat trays. It is helpful to use a pencil tip to trace the shape into the produce tray *before* cutting.

3. Glue the body, head, and wing shapes in the center of the sheet of construction paper.

4. Add dimension by pasting feathers, beak, legs and talons to the basic shape. Several layers will add visual interest. Paint the layered shapes after the glue has hardened a bit.

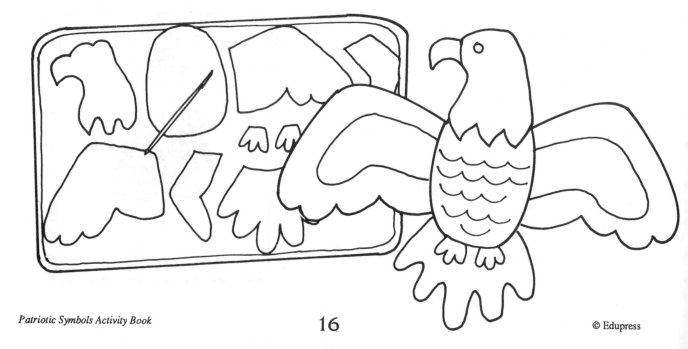

Commemorative Stamps

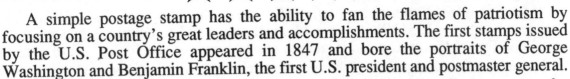

★ Historical Aid

A simple postage stamp has the ability to fan the flames of patriotism by focusing on a country's great leaders and accomplishments. The first stamps issued by the U.S. Post Office appeared in 1847 and bore the portraits of George Washington and Benjamin Franklin, the first U.S. president and postmaster general.

A country may also choose to honor an important event or famous person by issuing a *commemorative stamp*. The first commemorative stamp issued in the United States was in 1893. It honored the four-hundredth anniversary of the discovery of America and was called the Columbian issue. Another stirring patriotic moment captured on a commemorative stamp is the first moon landing.

Project

Work in small groups to create an original poster-sized commemorative stamp to display on a patriotic bulletin board.

Materials

- Poster board
- Crayons
- Scissors
- Magazines and newspapers

Directions

1. Divide into groups of two or three. Give each group a piece of poster board.

2. Look through magazines and newspapers for information about events and people that stir patriotic feelings. Brainstorm some ideas together as well.

3. Ask each group to select an event or person to commemorate in a stamp. Work together to sketch and color an oversized stamp to feature in a patriotic bulletin board.

4. Cut the edges of the poster board in a wavy pattern to resemble a postage stamp.

5. Invite each group to share the story behind their choice for a commemorative stamp.

Star-Spangled Bannner

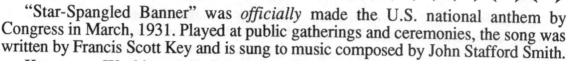

★ Historical Aid

"Star-Spangled Banner" was *officially* made the U.S. national anthem by Congress in March, 1931. Played at public gatherings and ceremonies, the song was written by Francis Scott Key and is sung to music composed by John Stafford Smith.

Key was a Washington D.C. lawyer sent to negotiate the release of a prisoner taken during the War of 1812. As he boarded the British warship a bombardment of America's Fort McHenry began. Key feared for the safety of those inside, but at daybreak he saw the American flag still flying over the fort. He expressed his excitement in a poem penned in just a few minutes. It was distributed on handbills the next morning and quickly became popular.

Other patriotic songs include *Battle Hymn of the Republic, Dixie, God Bless America, America the Beautiful,* and *Yankee Doodle. Hail to the Chief* is an instrumental piece frequently played to honor the President of the United States.

Project

Illustrate the lyrics from patriotic songs in a painting. Identify and learn to sing the patriotic songs from which the lyrics came.

Materials

- White construction or drawing paper
- Watercolor paint or crayons
- Song lyric sheet, following page

Directions

1. Photocopy the song lyric page and cut it apart on the dotted lines. Give a section to each student participating in the project.

2. If necessary, help each child read the lyrics. Encourage them to visualize the lyrics in their mind's "eye."

3. Students interpret the lyrics in a watercolor painting. Display the unique results in a bulletin board decorated with red, white, and blue musical notes.

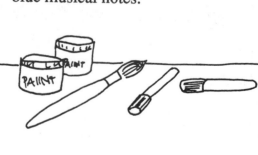

★ You're a grand old flag,
You're a high flying flag.

☆ O beautiful, for spacious skies,
For amber waves of grain.

☆ For purple mountains' majesty,
Above the fruited plains.

★ Every heart beats true
For the red, white, and blue.

★ From every mountainside,
Let freedom ring.

☆ Crown thy good with brotherhood,
From sea to shining sea.

☆ And the rockets' red glare,
The bomb's bursting in air,
Gave proof thro' the night that
our flag was still there.

★ From the mountains,
To the prairies,
To the oceans white with foam.

★ My country t'is of thee.
Sweet land of liberty.
To thee I sing.

☆ As I was walking,
That ribbon of highway,
I saw above me that endless skyway.

☆ I saw below me,
That golden valley.
This land was made for you and me.

★ From the redwood forests,
To the gulf stream waters.
This land was made for you and me.

★ Oh! say, can you see,
By the dawn's early light?

☆ You're the emblem of the land I
love,
The home of the free and the brave.

☆ Yankee Doodle came to town
Riding on a pony.

★ O beautiful for pilgrim feet
Whose stern, impassioned stress

★ Stuck a feather in his cap
And called it macaroni.

☆ I love thy rocks and rills,
Thy woods and templed hills.

☆ Thine alabaster cities gleam
Undimmed by human tears.

★ O beautiful for patriot dream
That sees beyond the years

Election Campaign

★ Historical Aid

In 1789, the Electoral College, a group of men chosen by the states, unanimously chose George Washington to serve as the first President. The right to vote and participate in government is the fundamental principal upon which the United States was founded. There are thousands of elections for Congress, state legislatures, city councils, and school boards held every year.

The center of an election is *campaign headquarters*. Here, volunteers distribute leaflets, prepare mailings, and perform many other tasks. Campaign headquarters is filled with posters, brochures and campaign buttons.

On election day, voters receive a ballot from an election clerk, vote secretly in a booth, then deposit the ballot in a ballot box.

Project

Convert a portion of the classroom into an area for completing projects one might find in campaign headquarters.

Materials

• Campaign Projects page, following
• See individual projects

Directions

1. Set up a work table in the classroom. Decorate it with bunting (see page 9).

2. Laminate and post the Campaign Projects page for students to review.

3. Invite students to complete one or more projects. Display the posters on the classroom wall and doors. Wear the buttons.

Campaign Buttons

Cut **white poster board** into 3-inch (7.6 cm) diameter circles. Use **marking pens** to color the circle with patriotic colors and symbols. (A real campaign, button would have the name of the candidate on it. This campaign button should spell out the letters U.S.A.) Put a piece of **double-sided tape** on the back of the pin and wear it proudly.

Campaign Leaflets

Fold **white writing paper** into three sections. In each section, use **crayons** to draw pictures, create designs, and write inspirational patriotic words that will encourage people to "get out and vote!"

Campaign Posters

Use **scissors, magazine words** and **pictures, and construction paper scraps** to turn a **large sheet of white construction paper** into a campaign poster that encourages people to be proud Americans and good citizens.

Be sure the poster contains a campaign slogan and patriotic images!

The White House

★ Historical Aid

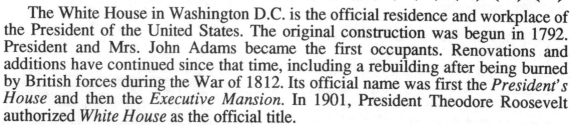

The White House in Washington D.C. is the official residence and workplace of the President of the United States. The original construction was begun in 1792. President and Mrs. John Adams became the first occupants. Renovations and additions have continued since that time, including a rebuilding after being burned by British forces during the War of 1812. Its official name was first the *President's House* and then the *Executive Mansion*. In 1901, President Theodore Roosevelt authorized *White House* as the official title.

The house has 132 rooms and stands in the middle of an 18-acre plot. The ground floor includes formal reception areas, the kitchen, and the library. The second floor contains the private living quarters of the President and family. The third floor offers rooms for guests, staff, and storage.

Project

Work with a partner to construct dioramas depicting different rooms in the White House.

Directions

1. Divide into pairs.

2. Cut apart the descriptive room cards and give one to each pair of students.

3. Create shoe box dioramas based on the descriptions on the room cards plus information gathered from reference books.

4. Share with other students what was learned about the different rooms in the White House.

Materials

- Reference books about the White House
- Descriptive room cards, following page
- Tempera paint in various colors
- Shoe or other similar-sized boxes
- Materials gathered by students
- Magazines   • Paint brushes
- Scissors   • Glue

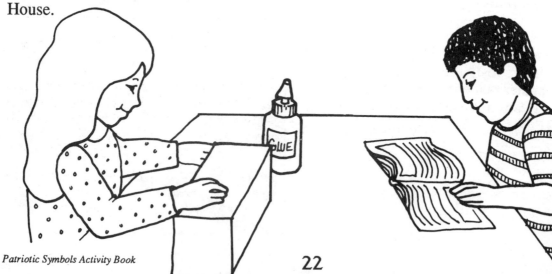

★ The Oval Office ★

★ The oval office is where the President receives his official visitors. Glass doors lead to the rose garden.

An American flag stands to the right of a large desk, the President's flag to the left. The Great Seal is molded into the ceiling and is woven into the blue carpet.

One wall contains a marble fireplace. Armchairs are placed in front of it.

★ The Blue Room ★

★ The Blue Room is an oval drawing room which serves as the main reception room for guests of the President.

A large blue rug bordered with a gold pattern covers the floor.

A large chandelier with tall lights resembling candles hangs from the ceiling.

★ The State Dining Room ★

★ This huge dining room can seat up to 140 dinner guests at one time. It is decorated in gold and white.

The marble fireplace mantelpiece is carved with buffalo heads. Over the fireplace hangs a portrait of Abraham Lincoln.

The table is decorated with a 13-foot (4 m) centerpiece of mirrors and gilded figures.

★ The Red Room ★

★ The Red Room is a parlor furnished with chairs and couches covered with red fabric.

The walls are hung with red silk edged with gold trim.

A large chandelier with tall lights resembling candles hangs from the ceiling.

A fireplace with a white mantle is centered on one wall.

★ The Green Room ★

★ The Green Room is a parlor filled with couches and chairs covered in shades of green.

A crystal chandelier hangs from the ceiling.

White and green drapes with gold trim and a large gold eagle at the top cover the windows.

The floor is covered with a rug in shades of red, pink, and green.

★ The Library ★

★ The library is pale yellow. Its walls are lined with shelves holding several thousand books by American authors.

From the ceiling hangs a red tole and crystal chandelier from the home of James Fenimore Cooper.

On the walls are five portraits of American Plains Indians.

★ The China Room ★

★ The China Room was set aside by Mrs. Woodrow Wilson to display samples of the presidential state and family dinner services. The collection was started by Mrs. Benjamin Harrison and is kept in glass cases along the walls.

A full-length portrait of Mrs. Calvin Coolidge hangs in the room.

★ The Lincoln Bedroom ★

★ This bedroom was actually Lincoln's office and cabinet room. It is decorated with a rosewood bed and a table and chairs that were bought while Lincoln lived in the White House.

Many souvenirs of Lincoln's life are here, including his rocking chair, his books, and a copy of the Gettysburg Address.

President of the United States

★ Historical Aid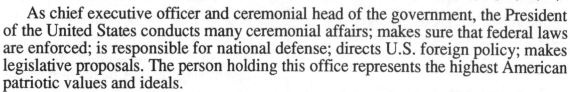

As chief executive officer and ceremonial head of the government, the President of the United States conducts many ceremonial affairs; makes sure that federal laws are enforced; is responsible for national defense; directs U.S. foreign policy; makes legislative proposals. The person holding this office represents the highest American patriotic values and ideals.

A 1969 law fixed the President's salary at $200,000 a year with an annual expense allowance and budget for maintenance of the White House. The President never has a day off and travels with a staff of speech writers, researchers, secretaries and policy advisers, and protective secret service agents.

Incoming White House mail averages thousands of pieces a day. It is read, summarized, and answered by staff members who report to the President.

Project

Write a letter to the President.

Materials

- Stationery template, following page
- Pencil or pen
- Crayons or colored pencils

Directions

1. Reproduce the stationery template for each student writing a letter.

2. Brainstorm and discuss places, people, and events that make children feel patriotic and proud to be an American.

3. Have them express these sentiments in a short letter.

4. Turn the paper over and illustrate the contents of the letter.

5. Gather the letters and send them in a large envelope to the White House. Decorate the envelope with stars and stripes to gain attention. Perhaps you'll get a response!

> If you're on the Internet, you can E-mail the president at president@whitehouse.gov

President of the United States
The White House
1600 Pennsylvania Avenue
Washington D.C. 20500

Dear Mr. President,

I am proud to be an American because _____

_____

_____

_____

_____

_____

_____

_____

_____

Sincerely,

Age: _____

P.S. If you turn the paper over you
     will find a picture I drew for you
     of something that makes me feel
     especially proud and patriotic!

School: _____

Capitol Building

★ Historical Aid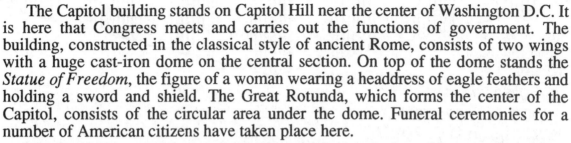

The Capitol building stands on Capitol Hill near the center of Washington D.C. It is here that Congress meets and carries out the functions of government. The building, constructed in the classical style of ancient Rome, consists of two wings with a huge cast-iron dome on the central section. On top of the dome stands the *Statue of Freedom*, the figure of a woman wearing a headdress of eagle feathers and holding a sword and shield. The Great Rotunda, which forms the center of the Capitol, consists of the circular area under the dome. Funeral ceremonies for a number of American citizens have taken place here.

The Capitol has 540 rooms, including visitors' galleries, offices, and reception rooms. Many rooms feature mementoes and paintings of the American past. There is also a President's Room, richly furnished with a huge gold-plated chandelier and portraits of American political leaders.

Project

Paint a historic mural similar to those found in the Capitol building.

Materials

- White butcher paper
- Tempera paint
- Paint brushes
- U.S. history reference and picture books

Directions

1. Look through picture and reference books, then brainstorm a list of famous and memorable events in U. S. history.

2. Divide into cooperative groups. Each group selects an event to depict in a mural.

3. Sketch the illustration then paint the mural. Feature the murals in a bulletin board display.

The Washington Monument

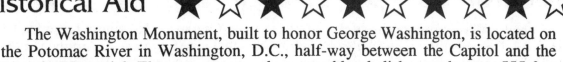

★ Historical Aid ★☆★☆★☆★☆★☆★

The Washington Monument, built to honor George Washington, is located on the Potomac River in Washington, D.C., half-way between the Capitol and the Lincoln Memorial. The monument, a huge marble obelisk, stands over 555 feet (169 m) high.

A memorial was planned to honor Washington while he was still alive, but he did not favor the expense. In 1833, the Washington National Monument Committee began raising funds for the project. The cornerstone was laid on July 4, 1848, with the same trowel that Washington had used to lay the cornerstone of the Capitol in 1793. Many persons donated stones for the construction, including Pope Pius IX who sent a marble block from the Temple of Concord in Rome.

Project

Make a stand-up model of the Washington Monument.

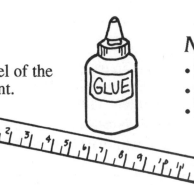

Materials

- Two large sheets white construction paper
- Scissors
- Ruler
- Pencil
- Glue

Directions

1. Fold each sheet of construction paper in half lengthwise.

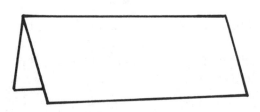

2. Measure 2 inches (5 cm) from the fold at one end of the paper. Make a mark. Measure 5 inches (12.7 cm) from the fold at the other end, and make a mark. Draw a straight line between the marks, then cut on the line. Repeat the steps on second piece of construction paper.

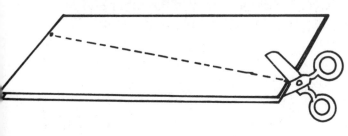

3. Fold in one-half inch (1.27 cm) on each length of the construction paper to create a flap. Overlap the flaps and glue them together, connecting all four sides to create a dimensional model.

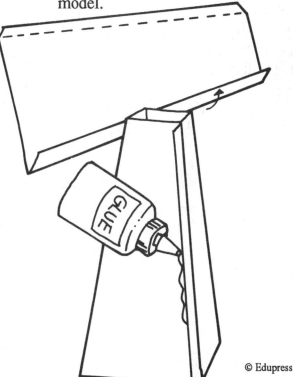

Washington & Lincoln

★ Historical Aid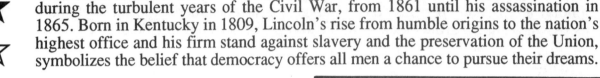

George Washington is called the "Father of His Country." No single person was more instrumental than he in the founding of the United States of America. For twenty years he guided a growing nation. As a military commander, Washington led the Continental Army in its fight for freedom in the Revolutionary War. As president of the convention that wrote the United States Constitution, he helped shape a democratic government. As a political leader he was the first man ever elected President of the United States in 1789.

Abraham Lincoln, the 16th President of the United States, served his country during the turbulent years of the Civil War, from 1861 until his assassination in 1865. Born in Kentucky in 1809, Lincoln's rise from humble origins to the nation's highest office and his firm stand against slavery and the preservation of the Union, symbolizes the belief that democracy offers all men a chance to pursue their dreams.

Project

Create mobiles that feature symbols representing two United States Presidents.

Materials

- U.S. map pattern, following
- Washington and Lincoln Mobile pages, following
- Red, white, and blue yarn
- Red, white, or blue poster board
- Scissors   • Crayons   • Hole punch

Directions

1. Reproduce the Washington and Lincoln Mobile pages. Give one to each child depending on the president he or she has chosen to represent in the mobile.

2. Color and cut out the pictures.

3. Punch a hole at the top of each picture.

4. Cut strips of yarn, one for each picture. Vary the lengths.

5. Cut out and trace the U.S. map pattern on poster board. Cut around the outline. Punch a hole in the map for each picture.

6. Thread the yarn through the hole at the top of each picture. Tie the other end of the yarn through a hole in the map.

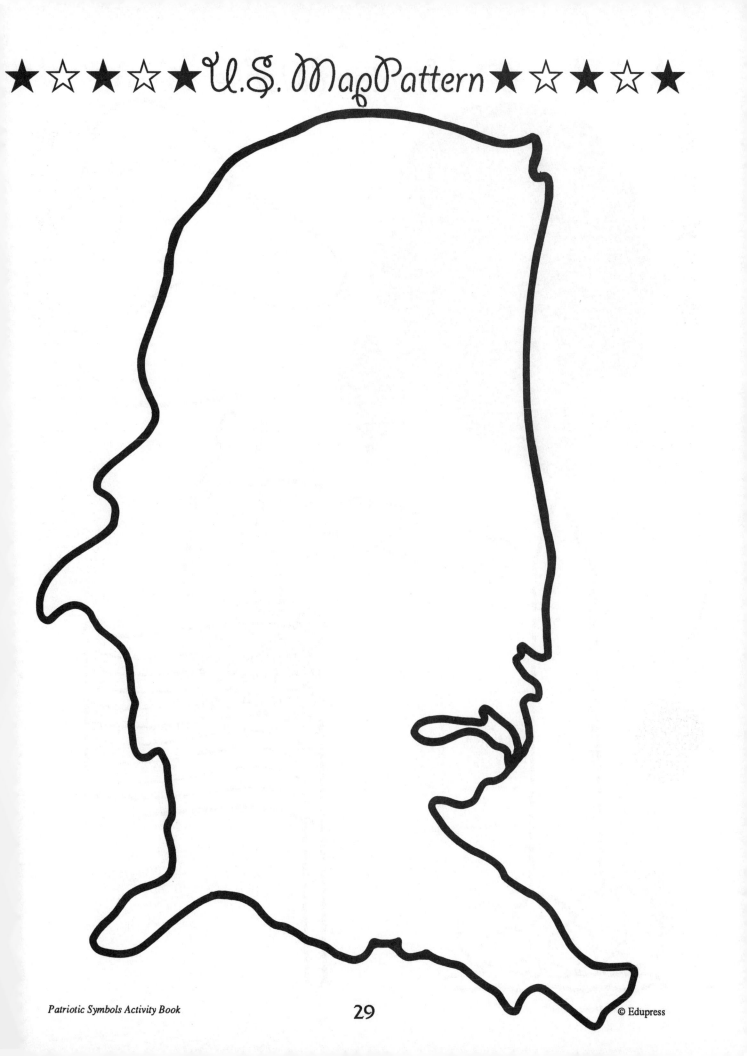

Statue of Liberty

★ Historical Aid ★ ☆ ★ ☆ ★ ☆ ★ ☆ ★ ☆ ★

The Statue of Liberty, a gift from France to the United States in 1884, is a symbol of American democracy and refuge for immigrants. The French people donated about $250,000 for the construction. The statue was shipped in 214 cases and assembled on Bedloe's Island overlooking New York Harbor. President Grover Cleveland dedicated the monument 1886.

The statue is an example of repoussé work, which is a process of hammering metal over a mold in order to shape it. Over 300 thin sheets of copper weighing about 100 short tons (90.7 metric tons) were used to fashion the statue. Liberty measures over 305 feet (92.96 m) above the base of the pedestal to the tip of her torch. Two parallel stairways, each with 168 steps, spiral inside the statue from the base to the crown. The crown has a 25-window observation platform that accommodates 30 viewers.

Project

Create a paper crown similar to that worn by Liberty. Memorize lines from a poem inscribed on the statue.

Materials

- Crown pattern, following page
- Large sheet white construction paper
- Aluminum foil   • Tape
- Gold spray paint or yellow tempera paint
- Scissors   • Pencil

Directions

1. Cut out the pattern.

2. Trace two times onto a large sheet of construction paper. Cut out and tape the two pieces together to form a circle.

3. Cover the crown with aluminum foil pressed into shape.

4. Spray with gold paint or brush with yellow tempera paint to create a copper effect.

5. Learn several well-known lines from a poem inscribed on the tablet in the statue's pedestal to recite while wearing the crown.

"...Give me your tired, your poor,
Your huddled masses yearning to breathe free,
The wretched refuse of your teeming shore.
Send these, the homeless, tempest-tost to me,
I lift my lamp beside the golden door!"

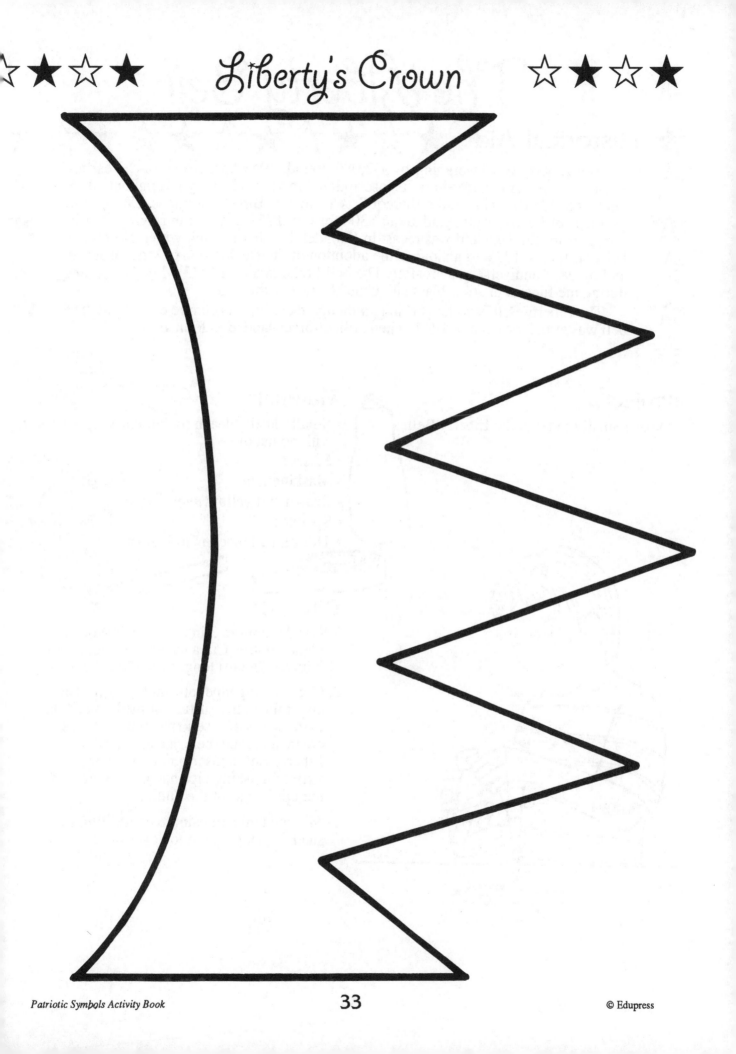

The Liberty Bell

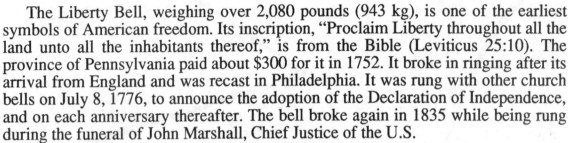

★ Historical Aid

The Liberty Bell, weighing over 2,080 pounds (943 kg), is one of the earliest symbols of American freedom. Its inscription, "Proclaim Liberty throughout all the land unto all the inhabitants thereof," is from the Bible (Leviticus 25:10). The province of Pennsylvania paid about $300 for it in 1752. It broke in ringing after its arrival from England and was recast in Philadelphia. It was rung with other church bells on July 8, 1776, to announce the adoption of the Declaration of Independence, and on each anniversary thereafter. The bell broke again in 1835 while being rung during the funeral of John Marshall, Chief Justice of the U.S.

The Liberty Bell is no longer rung, although there have been rare exceptions. The bell was struck on June 6, 1944, when Allied forces landed in France.

Project

Make a small model of the Liberty Bell.

Materials

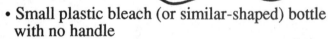

- Small plastic bleach (or similar-shaped) bottle with no handle
- Scissors
- Masking tape
- Brown and yellow tempera paint
- Sponges
- Thin-tipped black marking pen

Directions

1. Cut the bottom 3 inches (7.6 cm) off the bleach bottle. Cut a narrow wedge, about 2 inches (5 cm) long, from the cut edge.

2. Cut masking tape into short lengths and cover the entire surface of the bottle. Add extra layers of tape to the bottom edges to create a curved, bell shape. Write the Liberty Bell's inscription on a longer strip of masking tape and place it around the upper part of the bottle.

3. Mix the tempera paint to create a bronze shade. Sponge-paint to cover the tape.

Fireworks

★ Historical Aid

The colorful sparks and loud noises created by exploding fireworks are often associated with patriotic events and parades. Independence Day (Fourth of July) celebrations are usually capped by a display of fireworks, sometimes accompanied by patriotic music.

But most fireworks, also called *pyrotechnics*, can be dangerous because they are made by packing gunpowder into hollow paper tubes. Manufacturers add small amounts of special chemicals to the gunpowder to create colors. Most states prohibit the use of fireworks by individuals. The federal government also limits the explosive powder that can be used by individuals.

Project

Choose from two techniques to create artistic fireworks paintings.

Materials

- Assorted color tempera paint
- White construction paper
- String   • Scissors   • Drinking straws

Directions

1. Place three or more blobs of tempera paint on the construction paper.

2. Blow thorough a drinking straw to move the paint across the paper.

Directions

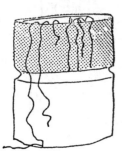

1. Fold the construction paper in half and open it again. Place three or more blobs of tempera paint on on half of the construction paper.

2. Cut the string into two-foot (61 cm) lengths. Coil a length of string over the paint blobs. Refold the paper. Place the palm of your hand on the folded paper and press.

3. With your other hand, pull the string until you successfully remove it from the paper.

All-American Food

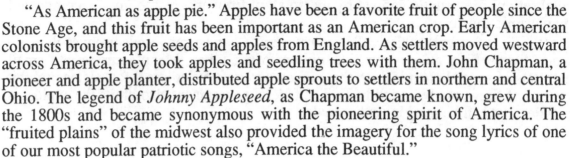

★ Historical Aid

The food and cooking styles in America are as diverse as its people. Regional dishes abound, while picnics and outdoor barbecues are popular holiday pastimes.

"As American as apple pie." Apples have been a favorite fruit of people since the Stone Age, and this fruit has been important as an American crop. Early American colonists brought apple seeds and apples from England. As settlers moved westward across America, they took apples and seedling trees with them. John Chapman, a pioneer and apple planter, distributed apple sprouts to settlers in northern and central Ohio. The legend of *Johnny Appleseed*, as Chapman became known, grew during the 1800s and became synonymous with the pioneering spirit of America. The "fruited plains" of the midwest also provided the imagery for the song lyrics of one of our most popular patriotic songs, "America the Beautiful."

Project

Cook in the classroom and prepare some food with a patriotic flavor!

Materials

- Bowls, baking pans, spoons, spatulas, measuring cups and spoons, plastic knives
- Recipes, following
- Additional utensils as per recipe
- Recipe ingredients

Red, White & Blueberries

Ingredients

Strawberries
Blueberries
Non-dairy frozen topping
    (Plain yogurt may be substituted)

★ Directions

1. Wash and pat dry all fruit.
2. Slice strawberries.
3. Layer ingredients in a clear plastic cup:
    Strawberries on the bottom, topping in the the middle, blueberries on top.

Apple Pizza Pie

Ingredients (for 6)

1 cup (236 ml) biscuit mix
¼ cup (59 ml) water
½ tsp. (2.46 ml) cinnamon
⅛ tsp. (.6 ml) nutmeg
1 cup (236 ml) applesauce
6 Tbsp. (89 ml) flour
⅓ cup (79 ml) sugar
¼ cup (59 ml) butter

★ Directions

1. Combine biscuit mix and water. Knead lightly and pat out into a circle on foil.
2. Spread applesauce onto crust.
3. Combine remaining ingredients to make topping. Sprinkle over applesauce.
4. Bake at 425°F (204°C) for 20 to 25 minutes.

Cowboy Beans

Ingredients (for 5)

1 large can pork and beans, including liquid
1 large can whole kernel corn, drained
4 hot dogs, sliced
1 medium onion, chopped
1 Tbsp. (15 ml) butter

★ Directions

1. Brown hot dogs and onion in butter.
2. Add drained corn and pork and beans.
3. Cook over medium heat until heated through.

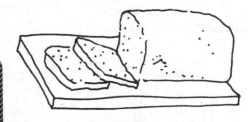

Easy Picnic Sandwiches

Ingredients (for 1)

2 slices bread
Spreadable cream cheese
Strawberry jam

★ Directions

1. Use star-shaped cookie cutter to shape bread slices.
2. Spread one piece of bread with cream cheese and jam. Top with second piece of bread.

National Holidays

★ Historical Aid

Many national holidays are patriotic. The President and Congress select those to be observed in Washington D.C. and by federal employees. Congress has also, on occasion, set aside special days to celebrate historic events such as V-J Day which commemorates the end of fighting in World War II. Some states observe Election Day (the first Tuesday after the first Monday in November) in the year of a presidential election. The governor of each state has the authority to specify the holidays it will observe. Several southern states celebrate Confederate Memorial Day some time in April, May, or June. Some New England states celebrate Forefathers' Day (December 21), and Patriots' Day (third Monday in April).

Project

Work in cooperative groups to create projects for a table-top display that features a national holiday or celebration.

Materials

• Holiday project cards, following
• Assorted materials based on the project selected by each group.

Directions

1. Divide into eight cooperative groups. Cut apart the holiday project cards. Give one to each group.

2. Each group assembles the materials they need to complete the projects on their project card and gathers further information about the holiday or celebration they've been assigned.

3. Arrange the completed projects in a table-top exhibit to be shared with classmates. Invite other classrooms to visit and learn more about patriotic holidays.

Martin Luther King, Jr. Birthday
January 15

★ Draw a picture of a dream, or wish, you have.

☆ Learn to sing a spiritual.

★ Make a paper collage with the colors of the human race.

☆ Make a banner featuring the word EQUALITY.

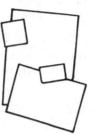

Presidents' Day
Third Monday in February

★ Make a rolled-paper log cabin.

☆ Make a poster board top hat.

★ Use tissue paper and starch to create a cherry tree.

☆ Fashion a three-cornered hat from construction paper.

Flag Day
June 14

★ Cover the classroom door to look like a flag.

☆ Use cloth scraps to make a red, white and blue wall hanging.

★ Decorate a star for each state.

☆ Color white stars. Paint blue watercolor over them.

Citizenship Day
November 12

★ Design patriotic stationery.

☆ Make a good citizen award.

★ Clip newspaper articles about good citizenship and create a collage.

☆ Design a quilt square using red, white, and blue.

Independence Day
July 4

★ Bake a birthday cake for your country.

☆ Paint a "firecracker-sky" mural.

★ Cut and paste magazine letters to create firecracker words such as pop, boom, crackle.

☆ Design patriotic gift wrap.

Memorial Day
The last Sunday in May

★ Use family photos to create a "memory" collage.

☆ Invite a veteran to share a special story on tape.

★ Make a bouquet of red paper poppies.

☆ Make a model battleship.

Labor Day
The first Monday in September

★ Make a shoe box diorama showing someone "on the job."

☆ Design a paper plate mobile that shows the future job you want.

★ Make a paper weight to give to someone who has a "desk" job.

☆ Make a magazine-picture poster of people at work.

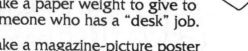

Veteran's Day
November 11

★ Make a banner that features the word PEACE.

☆ Listen to military marches.

★ Demonstrate a salute used by someone in the military.

☆ Use ribbon and stickers to make a medal.

Parades

 ## Historical Aid ★☆★☆★☆★☆★☆★

"Everyone loves a parade!" At least that's the way it seems in the United States! Political parades were especially popular in the 1880s and 1890s. Members of the U.S. armed forces often parade on holidays to show strength, conditioning, equipment, and skill.

Parades have evolved into community events honoring a particular occasion or federal holiday. They feature civic groups, government leaders, youth groups, bands, floats, banners, and flags. When a national flag is carried in a parade with other flags, it should always be on the marching right. On a float, a national flag should be hung from a staff with its folds falling free, or it should be hung flat.

Project

Plan and carry out a patriotic parade.

Materials

• See individual activities

Directions

1. As a group, plan the parade. Record your ideas on chart paper. Make final choices, then break down the plans into smaller, cooperative group tasks. Divide into groups and assign each group a job or let children sign up for the work group they would prefer.

2. Create a list showing the order of the parade. On the day of the parade, dress in patriotic colors and play patriotic music.

Plan a Parade Route

Plan a parade route.
Create a map that shows the route.
Make copies to send to all your guests. Indicate on the map where people should
sit. Assign class members to be in charge of
"crowd control" during the parade.

Paint Parade Banners

Create banners to carry in the parade.
Cut a piece of butcher paper. Paint patriotic
symbols or slogans on it. Wrap one length around a long PVC pipe.
Tape in place. Place a person at each end to carry
the banner in the parade.

Design a Float

Assign several groups to design floats.
The floats may be created on wagons,
boxes pulled by bicycles, or other imaginative transportation.
Decorate them with streamers, crepe paper, or butcher paper.
Be sure they represent the parade's theme!

Be a Color Guard

Learn to be a color guard and proudly
march with the national flag in the parade.
Non-military color guards include one colorbearer and two escorts.
When a flag passes by, the audience
should stand to salute it.

Medals

★ Historical Aid ★☆★☆★☆★☆★☆★

George Washington created the first U.S. military medal (decoration), the *Badge of Military Merit*, in 1782 to honor his soldiers for bravery during the Revolutionary War. This medal eventually became known as the Purple Heart. Other U.S. military medals include the *Medal of Honor*, the *Silver Star*, and the *Bronze Star*. Civilians can earn the *Presidential Medal of Freedom* for war services. The *Young American Medals* for *Bravery* and for *Service* are awarded to boys or girls under the age of 19.

Persons who receive decorations must meet certain standards. Most decorations are in the form of a star or cross, but some are round. They are made of silver or bronze and hang from a pin or from ribbons of different color combinations. Each has its own design and motto.

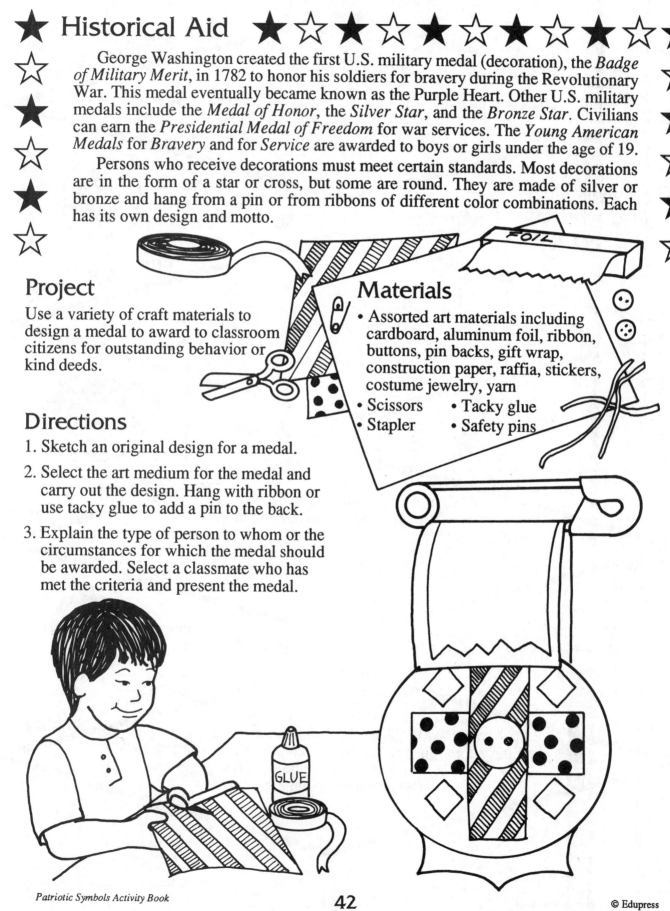

Project

Use a variety of craft materials to design a medal to award to classroom citizens for outstanding behavior or kind deeds.

Materials

- Assorted art materials including cardboard, aluminum foil, ribbon, buttons, pin backs, gift wrap, construction paper, raffia, stickers, costume jewelry, yarn
- Scissors
- Tacky glue
- Stapler
- Safety pins

Directions

1. Sketch an original design for a medal.

2. Select the art medium for the medal and carry out the design. Hang with ribbon or use tacky glue to add a pin to the back.

3. Explain the type of person to whom or the circumstances for which the medal should be awarded. Select a classmate who has met the criteria and present the medal.

★☆★☆★ Coloring Pages ☆★☆★

Project
Color or paint each page then choose from the ideas to create a patriotic symbol.

Materials
- Coloring pages, following
- Crayons
- Watercolors
- Scissors

★1 Stand-up Panel

Create an accordion-fold, stand-up picture panel.

★2 Picture Folder

Staple file folders together in the center. Glue a picture to each page.

★3 Wall Border

Place the pictures side-by-side to create a patriotic border for the classroom wall.

★4 Mobile

Cut out the pictures. Hang them with yarn from a clothes hanger.

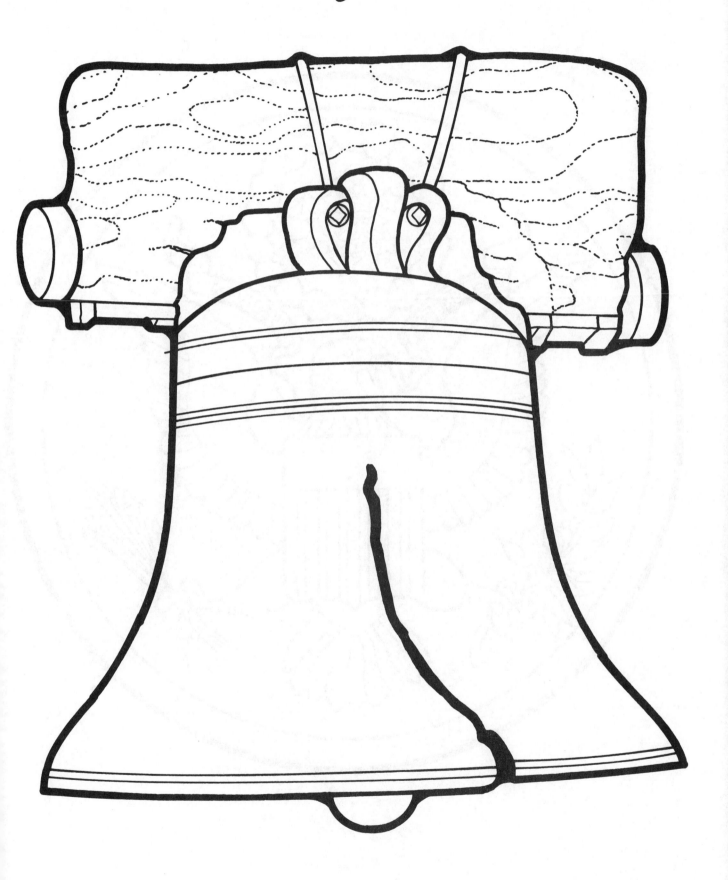

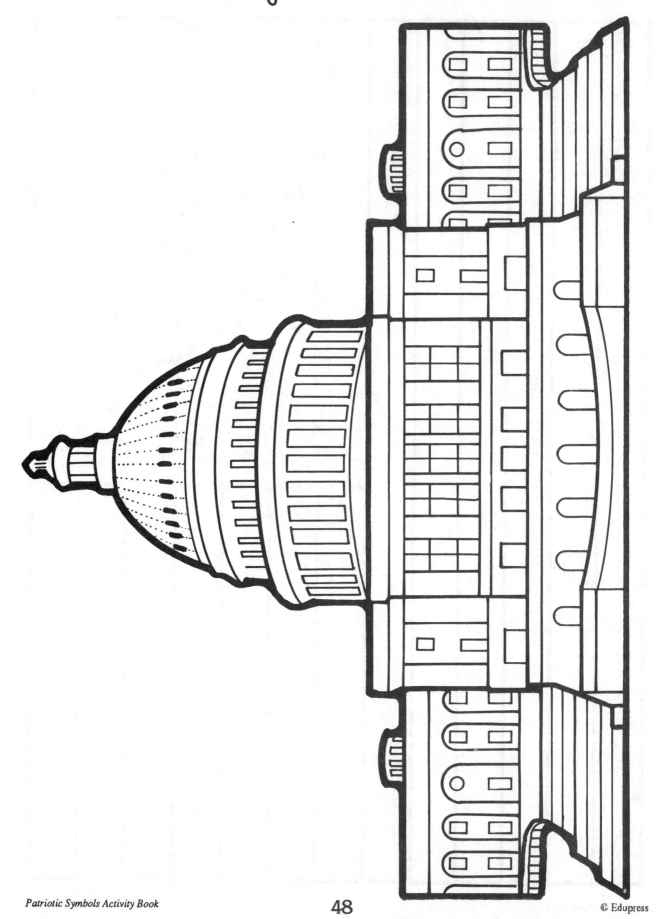